Fabulous Five-Minute Stories

A Lion Grows Up

Written by Sarah Albee
Illustrated by Joseph Cipolla and
Wendy Cipolla

Reader's Digest Young Families

It was a hot and windy day on the wide African plain. A group of lions, called a pride, rested on the sun-baked grass. One of the lions knew this was a special day for her. It was time to have her babies. Quietly, she wandered away from the group to find a safe hideaway.

It didn't take very long before Mama Lion gave birth to
Leah in a patch of tall grass. After a while, Leah's brother was
born. Leah and her brother weighed only about three pounds
each—much less than a pet cat! They were small, unable to
see, and helpless, but they would grow quickly.

Mama Lion knew it was up to her to keep her babies safe. They were completely dependent on her. Every few days she moved the cubs to a different hiding place, keeping them away from hungry hyenas and leopards. She had to carry them in her mouth very gently because they were unable to walk.

In fact, it would be about three weeks before Leah and her brother would be walking around. Until then, they would totter and fall. In the meantime, Mama Lion taught her cubs how to keep themselves clean. Mama's rough tongue was strong enough to lift Leah right off the ground! Licking each other's fur helped remove pesky insects, too.

Mama Lion took the cubs to join the pride when they were about two months old. Leah and her brother were excited to meet the rest of their extended family. There were cousin cubs about their age, older cubs, and lots of grown female lions, called lionesses. The lionesses helped each other take care of all the cubs.

Leah went right up to her father, with his rust-colored mane, while her brother went to meet his uncle. Their father and uncle were the only adult males in the pride.